Instructor's Manuals

VOIX FRANCOPHONES

MANA DERAKHSHANI
SAINT MARY'S COLLEGE

KATHERINE KULICK
COLLEGE OF WILLIAM AND MARY

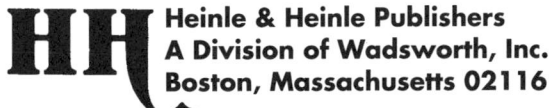

Heinle & Heinle Publishers
A Division of Wadsworth, Inc.
Boston, Massachusetts 02116

Your comments are important to us.

Let us know what you think about the *Bridging the Gap* program. The most important information we receive comes from instructors. Please send your comments and suggestions about the *Bridging the Gap* program to Heinle & Heinle Publishers, 20 Park Plaza, Boston, Massachusetts 02116. Or call toll free at 1-800-237-0053.

Your ideas make a difference!

Copyright © 1994 by Heinle & Heinle Publishers, Inc.
All rights reserved. No part of this publication may be reproduced or transmitted in any form or by any means, electronic or mechanical, including photocopy, recording, or any information storage and retrieval system, without permission in writing from the publisher.

Manufactured in the United States of America.

ISBN 0-8384-4609-4

10 9 8 7 6 5 4 3 2 1

Heinle & Heinle Publishers is a division of Wadsworth, Inc.

Table des matières

INTRODUCTION TO THE *BRIDGING THE GAP* SERIES — V

VOIX FRANCOPHONES
LE MONDE CONTEMPORAIN EN TEXTES — 1

VOIX FRANCOPHONES
DISCUSSIONS SUR LE MONDE CONTEMPORAIN — 35

INTRODUCTION TO THE *BRIDGING THE GAP* SERIES

KATHERINE KULICK

The *Bridging the Gap* content-driven materials complete the "bridge" between language skill courses and content courses by focusing first on content, with language skill development in an active, but supporting role. The texts and organization of these materials are clearly content-driven. While they are compatible with most upper-division courses in their focus on particular issues and themes, they are unique in their design to provide the linguistic support needed for in-depth examination of the subject matter and continued skill development.

At the advanced level, the *Bridging the Gap* program offers two coordinated content-driven textbooks in French, in German, and in Spanish. The two books in each language share a focus on the same set of topics in contemporary social, political, and cultural issues throughout the French-speaking, German-speaking, and Spanish-speaking regions of the world. Both texts provide substantive readings in depth as well as in length. Multiple readings on each topic offer differing viewpoints.

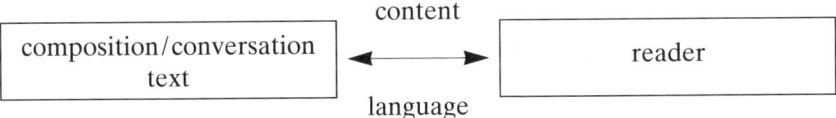

The two books differ in the skills they continue to develop. One book provides an emphasis on oral and written discourse strategies, while the other book focuses primarily on reading strategies. While each textbook may be used independently, when used together the two books offer an even deeper exploration of current cultural and social issues with a global perspective and substantial skill development support.

The readings in each book are authentic texts drawn from a wide variety of recent sources. Rather than presenting a sample of twelve to fifteen different topics and treating each one in a superficial manner, each team of authors has chosen to focus on five to eight topics in order to explore them in greater detail. All of the authors have agreed that the development of advanced level skills requires extended exposure to, and thorough exploration of, each topic. Detailed description, supporting opinions, etc., require a degree of familiarity with the subject matter that cannot be achieved in one or two class meetings. In order to explore and develop advanced level discourse strategies, an extended period of time is essential.

In addition to their focus on content, these materials are unique in their approach to skill development. Rather than simply recycling earlier grammatical instruction, these advanced level materials enable students to interact with authentic materials in ways that will help them acquire new skills that will set them apart from intermediate level learners.

As students leave the intermediate level and post-intermediate level skill development course to focus on literature, civilization, film, etc., we, as instructors, recognize the need for student language skills to continue to be developed even as the course focus shifts from language skills to content-oriented instruction. We would like our students to demonstrate an increasing sophistication and complexity in their language skills and in their interaction with authentic texts and documents. The content-driven materials in the *Bridging the Gap* series are intended to enable students to reach these goals.

CONTENT-BASED FRENCH: *VOIX FRANCOPHONES*

The content-driven approach presents an image of the Francophone world in its diversity. Content-driven teaching instructs students in a subject matter using the target language while teaching the language itself at the same time. While equal attention is paid to language and content, language is the means to an end, not the end in itself. This is an excellent approach for teaching language at the advanced levels: exploring a subject in depth requires that the language used to describe the subject be sharpened and expanded.

	Discussions sur le monde contemporain	**Le Monde contemporain en textes**
Unité 1	Les Enjeux de la Francophonie	Les Identités
Chapitre 1	Le Rayonnement culturel de la France	La France
Chapitre 2	L'Identité francophone et l'identité nationale: les profils multiples	La Francophonie
Unité 2	L'Environnement et la gestion de la planète	L'Environnement
Chapitre 3	L'Environnement: C'est l'affaire de tous!	Les Ecolos en France
Chapitre 4	Faire avancer le monde, sans faire reculer la terre	L'Arbre et le Sahel
Unité 3	Immigration: Perspectives multiples	L'Immigration
Chapitre 5	Emigration et immigration	La France face à l'immigration
Chapitre 6	La Voix des immigré(e)s	La Deuxième Génération
Unité 4	Religion: Traditions, evolution, questions	La Religion
Chapitre 7	Ce que croient les Français	La Religion en France
Chapitre 8	La Condition féminine dans un monde islamique	La Religion en Afrique et aux Antilles
Unité 5	Valeurs d'hier, d'aujourd'hui et de demain	Passé, présent, avenir
Chapitre 9	Au seuil de l'an 2000: tendances des Français	La France et son passé
Chapitre 10	Regard sur l'actualité africaine	Le Maghreb en transition

BRIDGING THE GAP

INSTRUCTOR'S MANUAL TO ACCOMPANY

VOIX FRANCOPHONES

LE MONDE CONTEMPORAIN

EN TEXTES

Content-driven Reading in French

MANA DERAKHSHANI

SAINT MARY'S COLLEGE

HH

Heinle & Heinle Publishers
A Division of Wadsworth, Inc.
Boston, Massachusetts 02116 U.S.A.

PREFACE

CONTENT-BASED INSTRUCTION   An increasing number of theoreticians and practitioners of second language pedagogy are advocating a content-based model of second language instruction that allows a more natural contextualization of language learning and fosters the use of authentic materials. *Voix francophones: le monde contemporain en textes* follows that approach by letting the content—the issues under discussion—determine the activities.

GOALS   *Voix francophones* is an advanced-level reader that provides students and their teachers with substantive information, presents stimulating issues for discussion, and fosters the development of higher order thinking skills while at the same time including some of the linguistic supports that students may still need.

In recent years much attention has been devoted to assisting students with the transition between intermediate-level language courses and upper-level content courses. The need for such articulation does not stop at the post-intermediate level. Students in their third and fourth year of French can greatly benefit from more systematic language instruction which will provide them, within the context of a content course, with the means to facilitate the transition from skill courses to literature, civilization, and/or business courses. To this end, *Voix francophones* offers a variety of advanced and superior level texts drawn from journals and magazines, scientific reports, and literary works within specific sociological and cultural content areas. All units begin with a reminder of basic reading strategies, and all texts are supported by advance organizers and pre-reading and post-reading activities.

COMPANION TEXT   This reader may be used in conjunction with *Voix francophones: discussions sur le monde contemporain* for a broader and more in-depth look at the themes examined here. Both texts follow the same thematic organization and provide a variety of alternative viewpoints revolving around the same issues. Both texts may be used in a third- and/or fourth-year college level Advanced Conversation or Composition course, in a Contemporary Francophone Culture course, or in an Advanced Level High School course. Most high school and college programs offer an advanced level contemporary culture course that revolves around daily topics (food, music, cuisine, etc.) that typically relate only to France and not to other French-speaking regions of the world. This course is usually taught as a content course, where students are expected to read lengthy texts for information. Often, however, students are not ready to tackle such readings without any language instruction support or guidance. The *Voix francophones* texts, on the other hand, bring to the content courses this linguistic support by systematically addressing the development of reading (in this book) and of writing and speaking skills (in *Voix francophones: discussions sur le monde contemporain*).

SCHEDULE *Voix francophones: le monde contemporain en textes* has been designed to be used either in a ten-week quarter or a fifteen- to sixteen-week semester course. Each chapter can be covered comfortably in four fifty-minute class periods. In the ten-week term, teachers may choose to cover only certain themes thoroughly by including all readings or to cover all themes but selecting only some readings from each chapter. In order to keep the francophone aspect of the readings, it is recommended that teachers address an entire unit at once rather than jumping from chapter to chapter so that both the French point of view and the view from outside of France can be represented.

ORGANIZATION In addition to providing a language support for content courses (such as a contemporary culture or issues course) and a content for language courses (such as an advanced conversation/composition course), the book offers for each issue discussed a look at France as well as at one or two other French-speaking regions of the world, thus opening up the French programs to a more accurate vision of French as a language of communication and transmission of culture around the world.

The text consists of five units dealing with (1) identity, (2) the environment, (3) immigration, (4) religion, and (5) past and present identities. Each unit is further divided into two chapters, one concerned with that issue in France and the other with that issue in other French-speaking regions.

Each chapter includes three or four texts, at least one of which is literary. The following features appear in all chapters:

- A short paragraph introduces the unit, followed by **Réflexion,** where students are asked to consider their own experiences and opinions on the topic of that unit. Studies show that people learn better if the new material can be linked to previously acquired knowledge, so this feature prepares the students for the texts that follow.

- ***Rappel des Stratégies de lecture*** works as quick reminders to the students to use the skills they have acquired in previous language courses to facilitate their reading. A different strategy is presented in each unit. It is assumed that at this level students know how to look for cognates, guess by context, recognize word families, etc. So there are no exercises connected with the strategies. However, each strategy presented is particularly useful in completing the activities in the unit it introduces.

- ***Préparation à la lecture,*** much like the ***Réflexion*** component, prepares the student for the following reading.

- *A Savoir* introduces the author and/or situates the text within its geographical, temporal, and cultural context.

- A series of questions and notes in the margin helps the readers think while they are reading, organize their thoughts, and react to what they are reading. This particular feature was designed to bring the second-language reading experience closer to that of the first-language reading. When reading a text for information that they would like to retain, most people underline key sentences and make notes in the margins. This feature tries to duplicate that technique.

There are various types of postreading exercises and activities:

- A *Vérification* section appears immediately after the more difficult texts as a means of verifying comprehension.
- An *Approfondissement* section prompts a deeper understanding of the issues raised.
- An *Observation* section asks students to look at particular discourse strategies and stylistic features in order to become more proficient at recognizing and interpreting them.
- A *Réaction* section elicits personal opinions and reactions.
- Some texts or sets of texts lend themselves also to a *Pour aller plus loin* feature, where the students are asked to incorporate outside materials, texts, or ideas to expand the focus of discussion.
- All chapters end with a *Discussion/Dissertation* section, and each unit ends with a *Synthèse*. This feature permits links to be made between texts that represent various points of view or aspects of certain issues.

It is recommended that the prereading be done in class before the text is assigned to be read and that the margin questions be answered at home. However, most other activities can be prepared at home for class discussion or assigned as written homework at the discretion of the instructor.

All difficult or technical vocabulary has been glossed at the bottom of each page; there is no lexicon at the end of the book, however, because students at this level must become less dependent on textbook glossaries and rely either on their ability to guess the meaning of a word from the context or to use a dictionary effectively.

The strength of *Voix francophones* lies in its versatility and its emphasis on integrating language learning and acquisition of knowledge in specific content areas. Focused on serious issues of interest to all, it offers a new platform from which the voices of the francophone regions of the world can be broadcast to students of French.

CHAPTER NOTES

PRELIMINARY NOTES

DICTIONARIES   Since some texts in this book require rather extensive and complex reading, instructors may want to take some time at the beginning of the term to teach students how to use a dictionary. Ideally at this advanced level students should own a good French/French dictionary, but that is somewhat unrealistic. Therefore students must learn to use their French/English dictionary effectively. They must be encouraged to read an entire entry with an eye to examples and contextual uses of the unknown word. They must also be able to recognize word families and roots of verbs. Some intermediate and post-intermediate texts offer a few exercises to help students acquire these skills.

PREPARATION FOR READING It is essential that students be adequately prepared for the theme of each unit as well as for each of the readings. The syllabus must allow time at the end of each class period to do the ***Réflexion*** before starting the next unit and the ***Préparation à la lecture*** before a reading is assigned. This is particularly recommended for longer texts that cannot be read in class.

MARGIN NOTES AND QUESTIONS Remind students that the margin notes are a tool for them to use as they read the text. Encourage them to write in the margins answers to the questions or any other thought that may occur to them while reading. These notes or questions will help them recall the text at a glance and provide them with the language to participate in the class discussions. Before the students do the post-reading activities instructors may want to ask whether there are remaining questions and difficulties. However this should not be an extensive response to the margin questions since the topics they address may be encountered in the post-reading activities.

EVALUATION AND TESTING *Voix francophones: le monde contemporain en textes* is a content-driven text, therefore it is recommended that any evaluation hold students accountable for their understanding of the content as well as the linguistic skills taught to support that content.

UNITE 1. LES IDENTITES

This unit centers around the notion of cultural, national, linguistic, ethnic, and individual identity. At the same time, it functions as an introduction to the concept of "francophonie" and presents several French-speaking regions and countries that may be unfamiliar to the students.

REFLEXION In the beginning of each unit ***Réflexion*** allows students to access their own notions and thoughts on the topic to be considered. On the first day of the semester, the questions in this section may be used as an ice-breaker.

OPTIONAL PREPARATION ACTIVITY Before starting the ***Réflexion*** discussion, tell students that you are going to call out names of groups to which people may belong. Then ask them to stand up if they hear the name of a group with which they might identify themselves or be identified. Start from the more general to the more specific. Here are some possible affiliations:

Americans	Europeans	Caribbeans
women	American Indians	married
men	Hispanics	single
Africans	South Americans	divorced
intellectuals	book lovers	artists
jocks	game players	cinephiles
sports fans	francophones	etc.

You may add any group that you think will make your students examine their identity and the stereotypes that are attached to it. Follow up by asking students to share how they felt about being part of these groups. Did they feel comfortable, uncomfortable, proud, ashamed, etc. The objective here is to rethink one's affiliations and discover which ones have been imposed upon each person and which ones have been chosen, as well as what the implications of this discovery will be when one is encountering new and different cultures and identities.

To discuss the *Réflexion* questions, put students into groups of three or four and have them discuss the questions. Follow up with a general class discussion about what each group has found to be particularly interesting, enlightening, or disturbing in their notion of identity. Students may be asked to brainstorm and put on the blackboard elements that enter only in one's specific identity as opposed to those that enter into a family identity, a regional identity, and finally a national identity.

RAPPEL DES STRATEGIES DE LECTURE Developing hypotheses on the meaning of what one reads and verifying those hypotheses are essential skills for reading proficiently. To practice them have students read a particular text in pairs, stopping after each paragraph in order to share their thoughts and verify briefly with each other their understanding of the text.

CHAPITRE 1. LA FRANCE

This chapter presents, through a variety of genres, how the French view themselves.

LE JACASSIN

PREPARATION A LA LECTURE Assign this activity to be prepared at home (or do in class) before assigning the reading. In class, spend a few minutes discussing the answers students have given. This may be done in a large group or in small groups. Make sure that the concept of irony is understood as it is essential for comprehension of the text. It might be good to ask students to give examples of ironical situations or statements.

LE JACASSIN The reading may be assigned as homework or be done in class. In either case the *Vérification* should be done at the same time.

If students have done the activity at home separately, have them share in small groups the classification they have done as homework and reach a consensus in their group as to the conclusions to be drawn. Each group will then present its views to the entire class. A similar procedure can be used if the reading is done in class. Students may draw up their list and classify it in small groups, or pairs then follow up with a presentation to the class.

APPROFONDISSEMENT This activity may be done as a class or in small groups.

OBSERVATION Have students generate a list of all instances of irony in the text while you (or a student) put them on the board. Compare these examples with the ones given in the *Préparation à la lecture*. This activity is an important stepping stone for the writing exercise in *Pour aller plus loin*.

REACTION This activity can lead to a nice concluding discussion of this text.

POUR ALLER PLUS LOIN This activity may be assigned as homework.
   Assign the *Préparation à la lecture* for the next text. Ask students to bring a picture typical of their region, city, or house.

HEUREUX QUI COMME ULYSSE

PREPARATION A LA LECTURE Elicit and put on the board a list of feelings one may have towards one's home when one is away from it. Have students brainstorm about ways in which one might express these feelings and put all suggestions on the board. Elicit a third list of concrete objects and places one might miss or that might symbolize one's home. Students may use the pictures they have brought to explain how it makes them feel and what elements in the picture are particularly typical of their home.

HEUREUX QUI COMME ULYSSE This is a good text to read in class rather than as homework since for many students poetry can be rather daunting. Make sure all vocabulary has been understood. Read the poem aloud and have students practice saying it in order to feel the sonority and music of the rhyme as well as the rhythm of the lines and verses.

APPROFONDISSEMENT Once the students have drawn up the list of elements and images in the poem have them compare it with the lists they had generated in the pre-reading activity.

OBSERVATION These questions as well as the notes in the *A Savoir* box may be used to introduce or review notions of versification in French.

REACTION This activity may be assigned as homework. Students should find it relatively easy to do after the preparation given in the pre-reading activities.

LES HOMMES DE BONNE VOLONTE

PREPARATION A LA LECTURE Bring to class (or ask students to bring) a map of the United States or of the students' countries as well as a map of the world. Have students answer the questions in this section in small groups then report back to the class.

It is important to do the pre-reading as a class before students attempt to read the text which may be somewhat difficult.

PRESENTATION DE PARIS A CINQ HEURES DU SOIR This text is short enough that it can be assigned along with the next Romains selection. The ***Préparation à la lecture*** will work for both texts.

The questions in ***Vérification*** (p. 11 and p. 16) are fairly simple and may be answered as a class.

APPROFONDISSEMENT (P. 11 AND P. 17) The class may be divided into five groups with each group responsible for answering two questions. Make sure you appoint or have the group appoint a secretary, to record the results of the group discussion, and a spokesperson to report to the class. Encourage the other groups to respond to the conclusions of the group reporting their ideas since every one has done the same reading.

OBSERVATION (P. 11 AND P. 17) The questions in this activity are designed to help students begin the process of analysis leading to an "Explication de texte." Instructors may want to use this opportunity to introduce some concepts in literary analysis, such as what is "personnification," "champ sémantique," "métaphore," etc.

REACTION (P. 12) This activity helps connect this text to the students' own experience and attitudes. This may be done as a class or in small groups.

(P. 17) Students are asked at this point to extract from their reading what they have learned about one author's vision of his own country and the identity of his people. Again this may be done as a class or as a small group activity.

DISCUSSION/DISSERTATION This activity is designed to offer more extensive speaking and/or writing practice.

Questions 1–3 can be combined to write an extensive summary and reaction paper or oral report about the readings in this chapter.

Question 4 should be a separate activity that may be assigned to groups for presentation to the rest of the class.

CHAPITRE 2. LA FRANCOPHONIE

This chapter introduces the concept of "Francophonie" and provides an introduction to several French-speaking countries or regions of the world.

Le monde contemporain en textes

CONJUGUER IDENTITE ET DIVERSITE

PREPARATION A LA LECTURE   Have students give names of French-speaking regions and countries and put them on the board. Then have students turn to the map (pp. 20–21) to locate each one on a continent and relative to each other.

Since many students may not know very many French-speaking countries, Instructors should plan to distribute or have students create a list of French-speaking countries and regions (with the correct article in French) using the map (pp. 20–21).

CONJUGUER IDENTITE ET DIVERSITE   This is a long yet relatively simple text. It can be assigned to be done as homework along with the *Vérification*.

In class the instructor should go over the answers given to the questions in *Vérification*.

APPROFONDISSEMENT   Questions may be done individually or in small groups.

OBSERVATION   Instructors may use this text to introduce the characteristics of an objective article, as well as review transition words and strategies that writers follow to structure a text coherently.

REACTION   Question 2 may be followed up by a class debate or discussion. Students (individually or in groups) choose a French-speaking region or country, with one group or students representing France, one group of students representing the United States, etc. The class, then, role-plays a session of the Association of French-speaking countries or regions. Each representative must have done some research and know what the country or region they represent would like to receive from the Association and has to offer it.

L'IDENTITE QUEBECOISE A TRAVERS LA POESIE

PREPARATION A LA LECTURE   The following pre-reading activities should be done in class before students are asked to read the two poems.

PREPARING STUDENTS FOR THE THEME   This activity prepares students for reading two French Canadian poems. Its purpose is to help focus on any previous knowledge students have about Quebec, the facts as well as the misconceptions and stereotypes. It is important to clarify and make students aware of the origins of such images.

Students may also be asked to think about objects, images, or texts (poems, songs, films, etc.) that seem to represent particularly well their own culture and bring to class any such object, image, or text. In small groups, in class, students share with each other what they have brought and explain why they feel it symbolizes their heritage. Each group can then report to the class any similarities or trends in the type of items they had brought or in the themes that these objects characterized. For example, if many people gave the national anthem, as an example, what would that mean in terms of the way they envisioned their own culture?

PREPARING STUDENTS FOR THE GENRE OF POETRY   Since poetry is often an unfamiliar genre for many students, instructors may want to lead students in a short brainstorming session to elicit categories of words associated with their own country, culture, or ethnic background. For example, first ask for any adjectives describing physical characteristics of it, then those describing feelings, then action verbs, concrete nouns, abstract nouns, and so on. Once several lists have been generated and put on the board, in small groups or as a class, students put together a text using the words on the board. After one or several texts have thus been created, discuss what is poetic about these texts and how they could become even more so. Introduce the importance of sound in a poem, what constitutes a rhyme in French, how is the rhythm created, what are alliterations and assonances, etc.

LE CYCLE DES BOIS ET DES CHAMPS   Read the poem to the students before discussing it.

APPROFONDISSEMENT   The questions in this section, as well as in the *Observation*, may be prepared as homework while students read the poem. In class, students share their answers in small groups or as a class.

The questions in this activity as well as the margin questions help guide the students towards a comprehension of the poem and an initiation to the process of an "explication de poème."

OBSERVATION   This poem provides a good example of traditional form with its "alexandrins" in four-line verses ("quatrains") and its "rhyme embrassée."

REACTION   Students should be encouraged to respond personally to the poem at this point and bring into the discussion what they had discovered in the pre-reading activity.

****

COMPAGNON DES AMERIQUES   This poem represents a more modern form and can therefore be more difficult to approach. Ask students to look at the text superficially to note how the appearance of this poem differs from the preceding one. Make sure they notice the lack of punctuation as well as capital letters. Remind them to use the syntax to guide them through the phrases.

Read the poem to the students before discussing it.

APPROFONDISSEMENT AND OBSERVATION   Students should be assigned to respond to these questions as homework after they have read the poem. In class, they may share their responses in small groups or as a class.

REACTION   Once again students should be encouraged to respond personally to the poem and bring into the discussion what they had discovered in the pre-reading stage.

DISCUSSION/DISSERTATION   Question 1 may be assigned as homework for more extensive writing practice.

Question 2 allows a discussion of the role of language in any definition of a culture. Students may be asked to think of other situations where language plays an integral part in one's identity and come to class with articles about language issues in the United States.

L'IDENTITE AFRICAINE A TRAVERS LA POESIE

PREPARATION A LA LECTURE Have students brainstorm on images that the word *Africa* conjures up for them and put the list on the board (or have students put it on the board). Follow up with a discussion of the origins of these images and of the extent to which they are stereotypical.

All three poems are short and can be discussed together in one class period. In the interest of time the class may be divided into three groups, each responsible for deciphering and analyzing one of the poems and reporting back to the whole class.

JE SUIS NE DANS UN VILLAGE Read the poem to the class. Have students point out Burkina Faso on the map.

APPROFONDISSEMENT, OBSERVATION, AND REACTION With this short poem, the reading and post-reading can be done in class, in small groups or as a class. The objective of the exercises remains to discover some of the ways the poet views his identity as linked to his land.

****

NEGRITUDE Read the poem to the class before discussing it. Have students find the Cameroon on the map. This poem may be more difficult than the preceding one because of the abundance of images and metaphors.

APPROFONDISSEMENT, OBSERVATION, AND REACTION This poem lends itself to small group readings because of its difficulty. Once again remind students as they answer the questions in these activities that the objective is to discover the notion of identity from another perspective.

****

RACONTE-MOI Read the poem to the class before discussing it. Point out that the poet is a woman. Have students find Ivory Coast on the map.

APPROFONDISSEMENT, OBSERVATION, AND REACTION The questions in these activities help students analyze the poem. Remind them that once again they are reading with the objective to gain another perspective or vision of the notion of identity.

DISCUSSION/DISSERTATION These questions lend themselves more to discussions than to written work although a summary similar to the one suggested for the French Canadian poems could also be assigned.

Have students generate a list of the features that stand out in these poems as characteristic of African culture and a list of the elements that enter into one's definition of one's identity in any culture.

SYNTHESE DE L'UNITE

The purpose of this section is to help tie together the texts in the unit. Students may be given a choice among the suggested topics or the instructor may choose one as a culminating written or oral activity for this unit.

RECHERCHES For those students who would like to extend their knowledge of the topic of identity beyond the covers of this book, this section offers a starting point for establishing a personal bibliography. Instructors may wish to use this section to assign extensive research papers.

UNITE 2. L'ENVIRONNEMENT

This unit focuses on the issue of the environment and the various approaches to the problem in France and Africa. The texts in this unit present a variety of genres, such as journalistic articles, and scientific and literary texts.

REFLEXION As in the first unit, this section is aimed at making the students aware of all the knowledge they already have about the topic. This preparation for the unit should be done in class before students are assigned any of the readings.

Have students brainstorm on aspects of pollution that are particularly worrisome in their region and list them on the board. Instructors may bring to class headlines from local or national papers (in English) dealing with issues of ecology. Alternatively, instructors may ask students to find such headlines to bring to class. Once many environmental problems have been identified, ask the students to generate a list of corresponding solutions, indicating whether these are currently being used or are only potential solutions. Also consider which ones involve the individual, the state, or the federal government.

In discussing why certain pollution problems are more important to students from certain regions of the United States, question 4 of *Réflexion* can also be addressed.

RAPPEL DES STRATEGIES DE LECTURE Prediction is an important reading strategy. Remind students that looking at a text in order to identify its type can be very helpful in setting up their frame of mind. For each text, students may be asked to glance briefly at the title and the source in order to determine or predict what kind of text they will be reading and what style they can expect to find.

CHAPITRE 3. LES ECOLOS EN FRANCE

LES PAYSANS REDECOUVRENT L'ECOLOGIE

PREPARATION A LA LECTURE Have students discuss questions 1 and 2 by generating lists of attributes given to peasants and farmers. Ask students to brainstorm on the environmental issues that concern farmers in particular.
   Questions 3 and 4 allow students to practice their predicting skills.

LES PAYSANS REDECOUVRENT L'ECOLOGIE After having done the *Réflexion* and the *Préparation à la lecture* in class, the reading may be assigned as homework along with the *Vérification* and the *Approfondissement*. Remind students to use the margin notes and questions as they are reading.

VERIFICATION Since these questions were answered at home, do a rapid check to ensure that there have been no misunderstandings.

APPROFONDISSEMENT In small groups students can discuss their responses to these questions and report back to the class on any consensus as well as any strong disagreement in interpretation.

OBSERVATION In addition to the transition words, instructors may want to spend some time analyzing journalistic writing by asking students what the opinion of the author is on this issue and how that opinion is communicated. Students can be asked to search the text for any sentence where an opinion is stated and then decide how they recognize it as an opinion. This may be done in small groups or as a class.

REACTION Students may be asked to prepare these questions, particularly questions 1, 2, and 4, in order to participate in the debate in the section *Pour aller plus loin*.

POUR ALLER PLUS LOIN Students should be assigned a role— such as small farmer, large agricultural producer, government official, representatives of the "green" party, etc.—in order to further prepare for the debate.
   An alternate activity would be to assign roles to students and have them write an editorial or a letter to the editor in response to the article they have just read.

DES ECOLOS PLUS VRAIS QUE NATURE

PREPARATION A LA LECTURE These questions may be answered in a full class discussion. Some of the answers may have already been mentioned in the *Réflexion* section and may only require a reminder.
   If time allows and students do not have a lot of information about the place

of environmental issues in the local schools, they may be asked to do some research on this topic and bring it to class for this discussion.

DES ECOLOS PLUS VRAIS QUE NATURE This reading is long and should be assigned to be done as homework along with the *Vérification* and *Approfondissement* sections.

VERIFICATION AND **APPROFONDISSEMENT** May be done in small groups or as a class.

OBSERVATION This section follows up on the previous *Observation*. Students are asked to look at the way the authors express their opinion in a journalistic style.

REACTION The questions in this section lend themselves to small group discussions followed by a report of the group's consensus or differences to the whole class.

POUR ALLER PLUS LOIN AND **DISCUSSION/DISSERTATION** Both these sections provide opportunity for a more formal synthesis to be done in written form or as an oral report.

L'HOMME QUI PLANTAIT DES ARBRES

PREPARATION A LA LECTURE Once again it is essential that this presentation and preparation for the text be done before students read the short story.

Have students work in groups to generate a portrait of the man based only on the title of the short story. Encourage students to be creative and detailed in their descriptions (age, physical traits, personality, clothing, habits, etc.). Each group will then present its portrait and explain the reason for each choice that had to be made.

Questions 2–4 may be done in small groups or as a class.

L'HOMME QUI PLANTAIT DES ARBRES This is a long text and students should be encouraged to read it without referring to a dictionary as much as possible. Remind students to use the margin notes and questions to help through this reading.

Assign the *Vérification* questions to be done as homework along with the reading.

VERIFICATION Students may be divided into small groups to share their responses to the questions before the whole class discusses them. Encourage students to use the portrait that they had created as a pre-reading activity to contrast with Elzéard Bouffier.

APPROFONDISSEMENT Divide students into groups and assign a different question or set of questions to each group. Determine or have students choose who will function as group secretary to take notes during the discussion and who will report back to the class the group's responses to the question(s) (this kind of structure for group work is recommended for most activities). Remind students that they need to find examples in the text to justify their answers. Have each group report back the result of their discussions. Allow enough time for a meaningful conversation about the text to take place in each group. Depending on the students' preparation the group discussions could last from 15 to 20 minutes.

OBSERVATION These questions lead students to focus on specific stylistic techniques and analyze some passages of the text as they would in an "explication de texte." Instructors who want more rigorous literary writing activities may ask students to use the questions in this section to write an "explication de texte."

REACTION These questions may help to instigate small-group or whole-class discussions about the text. Students should be encouraged to respond on a personal level to the character and the message of the text.

POUR ALLER PLUS LOIN In pairs or small groups, students should help each other choose the person that they are going to write about. Encourage partners to ask each other why they have chosen that particular person, how they can best characterize him/her, his/her physical appearance, habits, etc. By the end of this exercise each student must have a clear idea about the character he or she has chosen and a tentative organization for his/her article.

Encourage students to use the stylistic techniques of "L'Homme qui plantait des arbres" and imitate Giono's style in the article they are writing. Students may also be encouraged to include pictures or photographs in their article to enhance it.

DISCUSSION/DISSERTATION This activity is designed to provide a synthesis to the chapter. If students have been assigned to write the article suggested in *Pour aller plus loin*, instructors may want to use these questions for oral discussions in small groups or as a class. Again the questions may be divided among various groups who will, after discussing them, report back to the class what the consensus of the group was about that particular question.

CHAPITRE 4. L'ARBRE ET LE SAHEL

This chapter continues the theme of trees as central parts of the ecological balance of the planet. Here, the readings focus on the problems of vegetation in the Sahel, one of the ecologically endangered areas of Africa.

MILIEUX NATURELS AFRICAINS

PREPARATION A LA LECTURE   The first text in this chapter is an article written by scientists for a non-scientific but academic audience. Nevertheless it may present some difficulties because of the density of technical vocabulary. All such terms have been glossed at the bottom of the page, however students will still have to overcome a natural anxiety when faced with such a text. It is therefore essential to prepare the reading thoroughly.

PREPARING FOR THE GENRE   If possible ask students to bring articles in English about regions where animal or plant species are endangered. By skimming through the articles and/or brainstorming, elicit a list of reasons for the situation. Ask students to define what the stylistic characteristics of the articles in English are.

PREPARING FOR THE CONTEXT   If possible bring a large map of Africa to class so that students may see clearly what geographical areas are included in the Sahel. Review the names of countries that are located in the Sahel. Looking at the map have students guess what the climate of that region is, follow up with a discussion on the kind of vegetation that one finds in such climate. Brainstorm on the agricultural and pastoral uses of the land in that climate and on the dangers that its vegetation may face.

Have students read the first paragraph of the text and predict what the main point of the article will be. Then have them read the main titles of the text to refine their prediction. This may be done in small groups or as a class.

ORIGINE, NATURE ET CONSERVATION DES MILIEUX NATURELS AFRICAINS   Assign the text to be read at home and remind students to use the margin notes and questions to help them understand the main points of the text.

The text being difficult, you may want to do the *Vérification* section in class.

VERIFICATION   These questions may be done in small groups or as a class. Alternatively, you may want to divide the class in groups and assign a different set of questions to each group before bringing the class together for a review of all responses.

APPROFONDISSEMENT   The questions in this section may be done in class in small groups or assigned as homework. Question 1 lends itself to a formal writing activity, whereas question 2 may be better utilized as a springboard for a class discussion.

OBSERVATION   Students may be asked to refer back to the list of stylistic characteristics they had generated about the English language environmental articles in order to see what common traits appear in all articles about a similar topic, and what elements are construed differently.

REACTION   The purpose of this activity is to help students react to their readings and connect it to their own life of the mind. Follow up by having them list possible solutions.

POUR ALLER PLUS LOIN This activity leads the students to expand their newly acquired knowledge to other fields. Students may be asked to report on their findings in writing or through an oral report.

LE SAHEL SERA VERT

PREPARATION A LA LECTURE Many of the questions build on the *Préparation à la lecture* for the previous text. Knowing the type of vegetation in the Sahel and the dangers that threaten them, students may be asked to expand on the solutions they would propose to the government of one of the countries in the Sahel. Have students work in groups and present their plans for saving the Sahel to the class.

Questions 6 and 7 offer additional practice in specific reading strategies such as prediction and scanning for particular information.

LE SAHEL SERA VERT This article combines the political and economical aspects of ecology with the scientific issues. Ask students to read it and do the *Vérification* activity as homework. Remind them to use the margin notes and questions to guide them through the reading.

VERIFICATION Check comprehension by discussing students' responses to the questions.

APPROFONDISSEMENT The first question is a guided summary activity that can be done in small groups or be assigned as homework. This activity would be more successful if it is done after the *Observation* section.

The second question lends itself more to a class discussion.

OBSERVATION The questions in this section serve as good preparation for the summary in the *Approfondissement*. They may be done in small groups or as a class.

REACTION Have students discuss this question in small groups before sharing the result of their discussion with the whole class.

DISCUSSION/DISSERTATION Divide the class into two groups and assign question 1 to one group and question 2 to the other. Have each group share with the class any consensus or interesting conclusion reached in the group discussion.

Prepare the debate in #3 by dividing the class into botanists/biologists and ecologists and asking each group to prepare its case concerning the future of the Sahel outside of class. For the debate assign two or three scientists and two or three ecologists to each group. Each group should also have two judges who will decide the winners of the debate.

DU BON USAGE DE «L'ARBRE NOURRICIER»

PREPARATION A LA LECTURE   Ask students to think of fables and children's stories that they know. Put the titles on the board. Have students discuss what role these stories play in their culture then have them point particularly to those fables and stories that taught a particular lesson or moral. Have students point to those stories where animals played the main parts, and have them list the animals used most often in the fables they know and determine what characterizes each of them.

Have students do question 5 in small groups and present their story to the class.

DU BON USAGE DE «L'ARBRE NOURRICIER»   Assign the text and the *Vérification* for homework.

APPROFONDISSEMENT   Have students respond to the questions in small groups and report back to the class.

OBSERVATION   This activity is designed to introduce to students the notions of orality. Follow up by having students think of tales in English that include the technique of repetitions.

REACTION   Have students compare this tale with the ones that were listed in the pre-reading activity.

POUR ALLER PLUS LOIN   All questions should be discussed in small groups and may be assigned as group writing assignments.

SYNTHESE DE L'UNITE

The purpose of this section is to help tie together the texts in the unit. Students may be given a choice among the suggested topics or instructors may choose one as a culminating written or oral activity for this unit.

RECHERCHES   For those students who would like to extend their knowledge of this topic beyond the covers of this book, this section suggests a starting point for establishing a personal bibliography. Instructors may wish to use this section to assign extensive research papers.

UNITE 3. L'IMMIGRATION

This unit examines the experience of immigration from the point of view of the host country France and that of the immigrant. The second half of the unit deals more specifically with the second generation of immigrants in France and in Quebec.

REFLEXION Take a quick poll in class to see how many students have had first-hand experience with immigration or have a close tie to an immigrant community and how many have heard stories about immigration experiences in their family or among their friends. Have students brainstorm about the difficulties that may face an immigrant, put the list on the board, then elicit a list of feelings born of these difficulties from the immigrants' point of view and a list of difficulties and feelings generated in the people of the host country.

If possible, bring to class, or have students bring newspaper and magazine clippings (in English) dealing with issues of immigration in the United States. After having looked at these and discussed the issues linked with immigration in this country, have students brainstorm about which issues may be similar in France and which may be different. Determine whether certain aspects of immigration are universal.

Have students respond to the questions in the *Réflexion* in small groups and then share the gist of their discussion with the whole class.

RAPPEL DES STRATEGIES DE LECTURE Have students consciously practice this strategy as they read the texts in this chapter. Ask them to underline four words in each reading that they were able to decipher using the context, the word family, or the syntax of the sentence.

CHAPITRE 5. LA FRANCE FACE A L'IMMIGRATION

PENSER L'INTEGRATION

PREPARATION A LA LECTURE Have students respond to questions 1–5 in small groups as a first step then discuss each question as a whole class, asking each group to report on its own conclusions.

Question 6 asks students to skim the text to get the gist of the article. Allow them to elaborate a hypothesis as long as it is consistent with the first sentence of each paragraph as they skim them.

PENSER L'INTEGRATION Assign the reading and the *Vérification* to be done as homework. Draw students' attention to the note on page 102 about the recent changes in the immigration and naturalization laws in France. Remind students to use the margin notes and questions in order to better comprehend the text.

VERIFICATION Have students share their responses in small groups first and then in a large group. Compare the list of problems and difficulties drawn from this text to the one the students had generated in the pre-reading.

APPROFONDISSEMENT Have students discuss in small groups the solution proposed or implied in the text and decide what role the government agencies have to play in it.

OBSERVATION This activity focuses the students attention away from the content and toward the form. Have students complete question 1 individually, then as they report to the class their findings list on the board the expressions and verb tenses used to express other people's diverging opinions. All this should be done in class.

Question 2 may be assigned as homework or done in class with a partner.

REACTION Both questions in this activity require students to return to the issues of immigration in their own culture and country and compare it to the situation of immigration in France. Students may do this in small groups or as a class.

POUR ALLER PLUS LOIN Have students work in groups to create the questionnaire. The poll will have to be taken outside of class. The interview may have to be done in English. Ask each group to interview at least 15 people. The results may be reported back in writing to you (along with a copy of the questionnaire) or as an oral report to the class.

QUAND IL FAUDRA CHOISIR

PREPARATION A LA LECTURE This article focuses on the controversial issue of illegal immigration. The illegal immigrants were probably discussed in the last reading's activities. More thorough discussion and debate may be encouraged to make students think about this controversy in their own country.

Have students read the title and write an introductory paragraph on the topic on predicting the opinion expressed by the author.

QUAND IL FAUDRA CHOISIR ENTRE L'IMMIGRATION ET LA SECURITE SOCIALE Assign the reading and the *Vérification* to be done as homework. Remind students to use the margin notes and questions.

VERIFICATION Have students share in small groups their responses to the *Vérification* section.

APPROFONDISSEMENT Question 1: Have students create two lists, one for the left wing policies and tendencies and one for the right.

Question 2: Have students create two lists, one detailing the characteristics of the American immigration experience to which the article refers and one noting the elements of this experience in France. Encourage students to make a difference between the general attitudes towards foreigners and the governmental policies.

OBSERVATION The questions in this section help to focus the students once again on the form and stylistic characteristics of the journalistic genre. Instructors may want to have students compare the techniques used by the author of this article to express his opinion with those of previous journalistic readings such as "Les Paysans redécouvrent l'écologie" and "Des Ecolos plus vrais que nature."

Le monde contemporain en textes

REACTION Have students discuss these questions in small groups before coming together for a full-class debriefing. In order to provide more in-depth group discussions, the class may be divided into four groups, each responsible for one of the questions in this section.

Alternatively, the instructor may choose one or two of the questions for all groups to consider.

POUR ALLER PLUS LOIN Instructors may ask students to choose one of these topics for a longer written work.

Alternatively, students may all be asked to do question 2 as homework and come to class prepared to present their plan to their classmates. In class, students should be divided into groups where each member will present his/her proposal and defend it. The group will then vote for the proposal which will be presented to the entire class. Students may also suggest amendments to that proposal before they present it. Coming back in the large group, a representative from each small group will introduce the groups plan and take questions from the rest of the class. Finally the class as a whole will vote on the best plan proposed.

DISCUSSION/DISSERTATION This activity offers an additional capping exercise to summarize and synthesize the information in both articles. This should be assigned as homework or may be part of a test/evaluation exercise.

LE THE AU HAREM D'ARCHI AHMED

PREPARATION A LA LECTURE (P.112 AND P. 116) Remind students of the lists of feelings that they had generated in the *Réflexion* activity.

Have students brainstorm to elicit: 1) a list of adjectives, a list of concrete nouns, and a list of abstract nouns to describe the life of a young immigrant; 2) a list of action verbs to describe the activities of a young immigrant.

Have students discuss particularly the challenges facing children as opposed to adults in an immigration situation.

LE THE AU HAREM D'ARCHI AHMED There are two excerpts of this novel in this chapter. Both excerpts may be assigned and discussed at the same time. If the instructors chose to do both together, the *Préparation à la lecture* must be done for both readings at the same time. Assign also the *Vérification* section. Remind students to use the margin notes and questions to guide them in their comprehension of the text.

VERIFICATION Review rapidly the students' responses to these questions.

APPROFONDISSEMENT (P. 115 AND P. 118) Questions may be discussed in small groups or as a class.

OBSERVATION Have students underline all incomplete or short sentences and discuss their effect on the style.

After discussing question 2, instructors may want to assign the style imitation exercise in *Pour aller plus loin* or have students describe their campus or their neighborhood in the style of Charif.

REACTION   Question 1 should be done in small groups. Question 2 requires some personal individual thought before a group discussion. This may be given as a homework assignment.

POUR ALLER PLUS LOIN   See above.

DISCUSSION/DISSERTATION   The topics in this section lend themselves to a written activity for which students will have to synthesize the information they have acquired by reading the texts in this chapter. Instructors may want to ask students to choose one of the topics suggested.

CHAPITRE 6. LA DEUXIEME GENERATION

STRATEGIES D'INTEGRATION

PREPARATION A LA LECTURE   In discussing the students' response to questions 1–3, remind them of the discussions in chapter 1 regarding one's identity. This discussion focuses on the differences between the way one identifies oneself and the way one is identified by others (appearances, language, customs, etc.)

STRATEGIES D'INTEGRATION   This is a long text that needs to be assigned as homework. Remind students to use the margin notes and questions to help them achieve better comprehension as they read. There are only two questions in *Vérification* and students should be able to respond to these as they do their reading assignment.

VERIFICATION   Verify the responses to these questions in a large group.

APPROFONDISSEMENT   Divide the class in small groups to respond to these questions. Alternatively, you may assign a different young woman from the text to each group and have them report on her experience, giving as many details as possible. This kind of exercise would replace questions 1 and 2. The class should also address the issues contained in the other four questions.

OBSERVATION   Outlining a text is an ideal exercise to help students better organize their own thoughts. Have students do this with a partner. When they are done they may join another pair and discuss their outline with the other students.

REACTION   This may be assigned for homework.

POUR ALLER PLUS LOIN   Students will have to find someone in the classroom to interview. Remind them that a student with an experience studying abroad is an appropriate subject to interview. However, it is likely that there will not be enough such people in the class to complete this activity. If that is the case, ask students to find someone with immigration experience or experience living abroad to interview and report back to the class their findings and conclusions.

GENS DU SILENCE

PREPARATION A LA LECTURE

PREPARING THE CONTEXT   Discuss with the students the population of Quebec, particularly of a large city such as Montreal where various ethnicities reside.

Have students reflect of their relationship with their parents and generate a list of words, adjectives, and nouns to describe that relationship. Follow up by making a list of the conflict areas, of situations when they disagree with their parents, and the most serious topics of conversation.

PREPARING FOR THE GENRE   Elicit from students the characteristics of theater in contrast with prose fiction or the cinema. Point out the importance of the language and the sounds in theater.

Explain and review the few common elements of the French Canadian language in *A Savoir*. Ask students to guess what other linguistic features might appear in a French Canadian play (use of English words and phrases).

GENS DU SILENCE   Assign the text as well as the *Approfondissement* questions as homework. Remind students to use the margin notes and questions as a guide to easier comprehension of the text.

APPROFONDISSEMENT   Have students share their responses with each other in small groups.

OBSERVATION   This section focuses particularly on theater as a genre and asks students to think about the reasons for using it and what it allows the author to do.

Ask students to prepare in small groups one of the scenes for presentation to the class. Students do not have to memorize the text (although they should be encouraged to do so, if they wish), however they should work on intonation, gestures, facial expressions, and movements to communicate the character's true feelings.

REACTION   As a class, have students try to relate the experience of Marco Micone's characters to their own lives.

POUR ALLER PLUS LOIN   Students may choose one of the topics to do as homework. This activity may be done with a partner. Once the scene is written, provide an opportunity for students to perform it for the class.

DISCUSSION/DISSERTATION   Both these questions serve to tie together the texts in this chapter. They may be assigned as homework or used in a test.

SYNTHESE DE L'UNITE

The purpose of this section is to help tie together the texts in the unit. Students may be given a choice among the suggested topics or instructors may choose one as a culminating written or oral activity for this unit.

RECHERCHES For those students who would like to extend their knowledge of this topic beyond the covers of this book, this section offers a starting point for establishing a personal bibliography. Instructors may wish to use this section to assign extensive research papers.

UNITE 4. LA RELIGION

Religion plays an important role in shaping a culture or a society. This unit examines the role of religion in several French-speaking societies, in the first chapter in France and in the second chapter in Africa and the Caribbean. Because of the sensitive nature of this topic for some people, instructors should strive to create an atmosphere in the classroom where opinions may be expressed but without falling into judgmental attitudes.

REFLEXION If possible bring pictures of places of worship in the United States, in France, and in other French-speaking countries and regions. Ask students to try to identify the religion associated with each place of worship.

Questions 1 and 2 lend themselves to brainstorming by the entire class.

Questions 3–7 would work better in small group discussions followed by a general class discussion.

RAPPEL DES STRATEGIES DE LECTURE All pre-reading activities help students access their existing knowledge, of the topic and the text type, in order to provide a context and organizing principles for the new information contained in the reading. Students can be systematically reminded to use the clues given by the page setup or the titles to assist them in their reading comprehension.

CHAPITRE 7. LA RELIGION EN FRANCE

DES CURES PARISIENS

PREPARATION A LA LECTURE Have students think of names of clergy that they may know personally or have heard of in order to answer the questions in this section. Some students may not know any; encourage them to think about the function of such people in a community. The activity may be done in small groups or as a class.

DES CURES PARISIENS: A LA RECONQUETE DE LA FOI Assign the reading as well as the *Approfondissement* questions as homework. Remind students to use the margin notes and questions to achieve better and easier comprehension of the text.

APPROFONDISSEMENT Have students share their responses with each other in small groups and/or as a class.

REACTION These two questions lend themselves to extensive discussion and debate. Divide the class into two groups and assign a question to each group. After about 15 minutes have each group summarize their discussions and report any conclusions they may have reached.

POUR ALLER PLUS LOIN Students may be asked to choose between the first two questions, or instructors may assign both in order to provide students with the opportunity to see an issue from various points of view.

Activity 3 is a culminating exercise for this text. Students may use the letter in activities 1 and 2 in order to make their case for or against the need for the clergy.

LE PETIT CURE

PREPARATION A LA LECTURE Questions may be done in small groups or as a class.

LE PETIT CURE Assign the reading and the *Vérification* questions as homework. Remind students to use the margin notes and questions to assist them in their comprehension of the text.

VERIFICATION Do a rapid check of comprehension by answering these questions with the whole class.

APPROFONDISSEMENT Divide the class into small groups for this activity. Questions may also be divided among the groups.

OBSERVATION Activity 1 allows students to examine ways to express one's subjective opinion in descriptions. Have students make lists of words used by the author to talk about Jean-Paul, then draw conclusions based on the kinds of words and expressions that are most common.

Activities 2 and 3 are also studies in stylistics. Students may work in groups.

REACTION Questions may be done orally or in writing.

POUR ALLER PLUS LOIN This interview will have to be assigned as homework. Students may be asked to report on their findings and conclusions orally or in writing.

L'ISLAM: UN DEFI POUR L'INTEGRATION?

PREPARATION A LA LECTURE Questions 1 and 2 will allow the instructor to determine how much background information students have about Islam. Instructors may want to bring additional information about Islam and its place in French society today. Resources such as *La France en chiffres* and

Francoscopie will provide current percentages of the population belonging to various religious groups.

Question 3 aims at students' own perception of their religion or system of belief. It may be done in small groups or as a class.

Question 4 helps students predict the general theme of the reading. This may be done as a large group.

L'ISLAM: UN DEFI POUR L'INTEGRATION? The text is short and may be read in class. Remind students to use the margin notes and questions to assist them in getting the most out of the reading.

APPROFONDISSEMENT Have students work in groups to pull together their collective knowledge of Islam based on previous experience, class notes, and the reading and report back in a class discussion. Point out particularly the relationship between religion and politics.

REACTION This activity may be done in small groups or as a class. It is important to help students investigate their preconceived notions of Islam.

POUR ALLER PLUS LOIN Activity 1 asks students to examine fundamentalism as a socio-political phenomenon. Instructors may ask students to think about this topic in the world today and do some research in order to bring documents (newspaper articles, photos, etc.) to justify their opinions.

For question 2 have students bring to class the results of their research on Islam in the United States.

DISCUSSION/DISSERTATION This topic lends itself to a longer paper that synthesizes the information given in this chapter.

UN BEAU JOUR

PREPARATION A LA LECTURE Questions 1 and 2 prepare the theme of the poem. Question 3 prepares students to read modern poetry. All questions may be done as a class.

UN BEAU JOUR Assign the reading and the *Vérification* section to be done at home. Remind students to use the margin notes and questions to assist them in better comprehending the poem.

VERIFICATION Since these questions were assigned as homework, instructors only need to verify that there are no misunderstandings.

APPROFONDISSEMENT These questions may be answered in small groups or as a class.

OBSERVATION Have students make a list of the plays on words in the poem before discussing what function they have. Point out that a study of the rhyme will reveal more plays on words.

REACTION Discuss these questions in small groups and have students report back the result of their group consultations to the class.

POUR ALLER PLUS LOIN Either question may be assigned for additional written work.

Alternately, students who are more kinetic or artistic may be asked to perform the scene for the class or to draw a sketch of the scene.

DISCUSSION/DISSERTATION Students may be given a choice of topic for a longer written work that will allow them to synthesize the information and insight they have acquired in reading the texts in this chapter.

CHAPITRE 8. LA RELIGION EN AFRIQUE ET AUX ANTILLES

QUAND ALLAH EST NOIR

PREPARATION A LA LECTURE Questions 1 and 2 prepare the theme of the first reading. Question 3 asks students to skim the questions in the interview and predict the answers. All three questions may be done as a class.

QUAND ALLAH EST NOIR Ask students to read the text for homework. Remind students to use the margin questions and notes to help them better comprehend the text.

APPROFONDISSEMENT Have students respond to the questions in small groups and report back their answers in a large class discussion.

REACTION The class may be divided into two groups with each group responsible for one of the topics in this section. Follow up by having each group report on its discussion and conclusions.

POUR ALLER PLUS LOIN This may be assigned if students and instructors want an opportunity to discover more about the religions in Africa. It can also serve as an introduction to the following reading.

LE SOUFFLE DES ANCETRES

PREPARATION A LA LECTURE Questions 1–3 may be done in small groups to prepare students for the content of the reading.

For question 3, instructors may have to give one or two examples of events, such as getting a driver's license, going on a date, etc., that mark the passage from childhood to adulthood.

Question 4 may be done as a class with a more detailed map of Africa.

LE SOUFFLE DES ANCETRES   This reading is long and may present some difficulties. Assign it and the *Vérification* section as homework and remind students to use the margin notes and questions in order to achieve a better understanding of the text.

VERIFICATION   Go over these questions as a class and verify that the text has been understood.

APPROFONDISSEMENT   Divide the class into five small groups and assign two questions to each group. After some small group discussion, ask each group to report their conclusions to the class.

OBSERVATION   This activity may be assigned as homework or may be done in class in order to give students more focused writing practice.

REACTION   These discussion questions may be done in small groups or as a class.

POUR ALLER PLUS LOIN   Students may be asked to report on their research in writing or orally.

PLUIE ET VENT SUR TELUMEE MIRACLE

PREPARATION A LA LECTURE   Bring a map of the Caribbean islands or a large world map to class and point out Martinique and Guadeloupe. If such maps are not available, refer students to the map on pp. 20–21 in order to locate these islands.

Have students read the introductory paragraph and answer the questions in small groups or as a class.

PLUIE ET VENT SUR TELUMEE MIRACLE   Assign the reading as well as the *Vérification* section for homework. Remind students to use the margin notes and questions in order to achieve a better comprehension of the text.

VERIFICATION   Go over these questions as a class and verify that the text has been understood.

APPROFONDISSEMENT   Divide the class into six groups and assign a question to each group. When the class reassembles to hear the group reports, encourage all students to participate in the discussion.

REACTION   These questions may be discussed in small groups or as a class.

POUR ALLER PLUS LOIN   Ask students first to bring to class the research, readings, etc. required to complete this writing assignment. Have them share these with a partner or in a small group in order to get feedback from their classmates about ways to organize their paper and draw their conclusions.

LA SAUNERIE DE LA VIEILLE D'AMAFI

PREPARATION A LA LECTURE Have students list legendary and mythological figures and write these on the blackboard. Ask students to determine to which tradition each one is attached and what function the legends and myths have in that tradition.

LA SAUNERIE DE LA VIEILLE D'AMAFI Assign the reading and the *Vérification* section as homework. Remind students to use the margin notes and questions to achieve a better comprehension of the text.

VERIFICATION Have students discuss their answers in small groups before the class discussion.

APPROFONDISSEMENT These questions may be addressed in small groups or as a class.

OBSERVATION The questions in this activity may be assigned as homework or be done in small groups or as a class.

REACTION Students have to return to the pre-reading activities in order to compare this legend to ones that they know in their own tradition.

POUR ALLER PLUS LOIN For activity 2 in this section, have students work in small groups to create a legend. Encourage them to add characteristics of oral tradition. In a second stage, have students present their legend orally to the rest of the class.

DISCUSSION/DISSERTATION The first topic asks students to create a chart or a list of religions present in Africa and the Caribbean including particular characteristics such as the role of each religion in the political and public arena.

The second topic lends itself to a written summary of the information students have acquired in this chapter.

SYNTHESE DE L'UNITE

The purpose of this section is to help tie together the texts in the unit. Students may be given a choice among the suggested topics or instructors may choose one as a culminating written or oral activity for this unit.

RECHERCHES For those students who would like to extend their knowledge of this topic beyond the covers of this book, this section offers a starting point for establishing a personal bibliography. Instructors may wish to use this section to assign extensive research papers.

UNITE 5. PASSE, PRESENT, AVENIR

Having started with some definitions of individual, national, and cultural identity, the book ends with a look at how certain identities, each in its own way, negotiate the passage of time and greet the future from the vision of their past. On one hand France is reevaluating and redefining its history and its place in the world; on the other the North African countries are breaking away from their tradition towards a modernity that does not reject the past but values it.

REFLEXION   All the questions in this section deal with perception of the past and its impact on the present and the future. Have students respond to these questions in small groups before coming together as a class for a general discussion.

RAPPEL DES STRATEGIES DE LECTURE   Remind students to take a quick look at a text before starting to read it in order to get a feel for its organization. In addition, point out that the short introductions before each text, the pre-reading activities, as well as the margin notes provide the cultural context needed to achieve better comprehension.

CHAPITRE 9. LA FRANCE ET SON PASSE

UN MAL FRANÇAIS DANS NOS TETES!

PREPARATION A LA LECTURE   Have students respond to the questions in small groups and report their conclusions to the class.

UN MAL FRANÇAIS DANS NOS TETES!   Assign the text and the *Approfondissement* section as homework. Remind students to use the margin notes and questions to assist them in understanding the text and its cultural context.

APPROFONDISSEMENT   In small groups, have students discuss with each other their individual answers to the questions in order to compose a group response to each question. Choose a person from each group to present the answer to one question. Encourage all other students to participate in the general discussion as they listen to their classmates' reports.

OBSERVATION   Question 1 asks students to look once again at the way in which a writer expresses an opinion. Encourage students to create a personal list of vocabulary and expressions for their own future use.

Question 2 asks students to observe the presentation and development of a thesis. Once this analysis has been done, students may be asked to write a short paragraph modeled on this pattern.

REACTION   Both questions may be used for oral discussion or written work.

HIER, C'EST TOUJOURS LA BELLE EPOQUE

PREPARATION A LA LECTURE   Students can consider the questions in this section individually or with a partner before a general class discussion.

HIER, C'EST TOUJOURS LA BELLE EPOQUE   Assign the reading and the *Approfondissement* section as homework. Remind students to use the margin notes and questions.

APPROFONDISSEMENT   Have a general discussion based on the students' responses to the questions in this section.

OBSERVATION   The activities in this section may be done in small groups or individually before a general class discussion.

REACTION   Question 2 lends itself to a longer written work that may be assigned for homework.

POUR ALLER PLUS LOIN   Students are asked to prepare a questionnaire for an interview. In the first stage, students create the questionnaire in small groups in class. The second and third stage of this activity may be done outside of class. Encourage students to seek French-speaking persons to interview. Students hand in a copy of their questionnaire as well as a summary of their results. You may choose to ask each group or each student to hand in a complete project.

LA DERIVE DES SENTIMENTS

PREPARATION A LA LECTURE   Whether these questions are answered individually or in small groups, a general class discussion is important before students read the text.

LA DERIVE DES SENTIMENTS   Since the readings on pages 204–205, 206–208, and 209–210 are short and all are excerpts of one novel, instructors may choose to assign them all at once. If this is done, the *Approfondissement* sections may be assigned at the same time. Remind students to use the margins notes and questions.

APPROFONDISSEMENT (P. 205, P. 208, AND P. 210)   Divide the class into three groups each responsible for one of the excerpts. The groups will be given a set time limit to coordinate their responses to the questions relating to their excerpt. Each group will present the excerpt that they discussed to the class. Encourage other students to agree, disagree, or ask questions after each presentation.

OBSERVATION (P. 206 AND P. 208)   Both sections of *Observation* may be handled in the same manner as the *Approfondissement*.

REACTION (P. 206, P. 208, AND P. 211) After a discussion of the *Approfondissement* sections, encourage students to use the questions in the *Réaction* sections to express personal feelings and thoughts generated by these readings.

DISCUSSION/DISSERTATION Questions 1 and 2 may be used for follow-up discussions and syntheses. Questions 3 and 4 may be used for longer written assignments.

CHAPITRE 10. LE MAGHREB EN TRANSITION

TUNIS, LES MOUSQUETAIRES DU BEY

PREPARATION A LA LECTURE Before discussing the questions in this section in class, ask students to bring pictures of typical architectural styles from their hometown or region, from famous American cities, or pictures of a space that reflects their personality (such as their room, or their house, etc.).

In small groups, have students describe the pictures they have brought and analyze what features of a culture or an individual's personality are reflected in that architecture or decoration.

TUNIS, LES MOUSQUETAIRES DU BEY Assign the reading and the *Approfondissement* section for homework. Remind students to use the margin notes and questions.

APPROFONDISSEMENT In small groups, have students discuss with each other their individual answers to the questions in order to compose a group response to each question. Choose a person from each group to present the answer to one question. Encourage all other students to participate in the general discussion as they listen to their classmates' reports.

OBSERVATION Have students respond to the questions in this section in a general class discussion.

REACTION Follow-up activity: Have students plan an imaginary visit to Tunis and describe it orally or in writing.

POUR ALLER PLUS LOIN This activity is an expansion on the pre-reading activity. Because it may be difficult for the students to find the needed information, allow them to work in groups and hand in one group homework.

ELEVEE DANS UN HAREM

PREPARATION A LA LECTURE Have students brainstorm as a class on the questions they would ask a woman who had lived in a harem.

Students may respond to questions 2–4 in small groups before a general class discussion.

ELEVEE DANS UN HAREM Assign the reading and the *Vérification* section for homework. Remind students to use the margin notes and questions.

VERIFICATION Verify comprehension by answering the questions with the entire class.

APPROFONDISSEMENT Divide the class into six groups and assign a question to each group. After a set time, have a person from each group summarize and explain the groups' response to that question. Encourage discussion from other students.

OBSERVATION This may be assigned as homework or done in class for written practice.

REACTION The questions in this section may be discussed in small groups or as a class.

POUR ALLER PLUS LOIN This topic may be assigned for a longer paper. Alternatively, students may write a possible interview with a pioneer woman telling about her life.

FEMMES D'ALGER

PREPARATION A LA LECTURE Questions in this section may be discussed in small groups or as a class. Instructors may want to prepare a more extensive account of the history of Algeria and its independence war for a mini-lecture.

FEMMES D'ALGER DANS LEUR APPARTEMENT Assign reading and *Vérification* section. Remind students to use the margin notes and questions.

VERIFICATION Discuss the answers to the questions in this section as a class.

APPROFONDISSEMENT Have students respond to the questions in this section in small groups before reporting their conclusions to the class.

OBSERVATION May be done in small groups or as a class.

REACTION The questions in this section lend themselves to either small group discussions or written work.

POUR ALLER PLUS LOIN Have students prepare the questionnaire in small groups before going outside of class for the actual interviews.

SYNTHESE DE L'UNITE

The purpose of this section is to help tie together the texts in the unit. Students may be given a choice among the suggested topics or instructors may choose one as a culminating written or oral activity for this unit.

RECHERCHES For those students who would like to extend their knowledge of this topic beyond the covers of this book, this section offers a starting point for establishing a personal bibliography. Instructors may wish to use this section to assign extensive research papers.

Bridging The Gap

INSTRUCTOR'S MANUAL TO ACCOMPANY

VOIX FRANCOPHONES

DISCUSSIONS SUR LE MONDE CONTEMPORAIN

Content-driven Conversation and Composition in French

KATHERINE M. KULICK
COLLEGE OF WILLIAM AND MARY

HH

Heinle & Heinle Publishers
A Division of Wadsworth, Inc.
Boston, Massachusetts 02116 U.S.A.

INTRODUCTION

Voix francophones: discussions sur le monde contemporain is a unique, student-centered textbook focusing on contemporary social and cultural issues in the Francophone world. A content-driven textbook for conversation, composition, combined composition/conversation courses, or a cultural supplement for Francophone literature and culture courses, *Voix francophones* uses authentic texts to explore current issues while providing the linguistic support necessary for students to operate at this sophisticated level. It is intended for third- or fourth-year college students or fifth-year high school students. It offers the opportunity for in-depth exploration of five major issues in contemporary society.

Voix francophones addresses two very pressing needs:

1. *Voix francophones* responds to the need for up-to-date, authentic materials on contemporary issues in the Francophone world. The title reflects an important decision to provide multiple viewpoints on each issue presented and to let each group or region represented speak for itself.

2. *Voix francophones* also responds to the need for linguistic support at the discourse level for advanced courses in French conversation, composition, and combined composition and conversation. The oral and written strategies described in *Voix francophones,* which are taken from textbooks for young French-speakers, offer concise explanations or schematic outlines.

UNIQUE FEATURES Teachers of advanced-level conversation and composition courses frequently note that in order to develop appropriate discourse strategies students need a degree of familiarity with the subject matter (new vocabulary, understanding of concepts, etc.) that cannot be achieved in two or three class meetings. In order to fully explore diverse points of view and to go beyond a superficial discussion, students need an extended period of time to explore each topic. By touching upon few topics, but going into greater depth, *Voix francophones* gives students the opportunity to fully develop their ideas, to present them orally or in writing, and to revise their original theses.

Voix francophones focuses on five main themes, each of which is the focus of oral and written discussion for three weeks in a fifteen-week semester or two weeks in a ten-week quarter.

> Unité 1: Les Enjeux de la Francophonie
> Unité 2: L'Environnement et la gestion de la planète
> Unité 3: Immigration: Perspectives multiples
> Unité 4: Religion: Traditions, évolution, questions
> Unité 5: Valeurs d'hier, d'aujourd'hui et de demain

Each unit is divided into two chapters. The first chapter addresses the unit theme from a French (France) perspective. The second chapter of each unit focuses on the same theme but offers the point of view of writers from Quebec, the Maghreb, the Antilles, or a particular country within Francophone Africa.

The style of the texts is varied, including articles from magazines and newspapers, government reports and documents, as well as literary selections. (See the coordinated reader, *Voix francophones: le monde contemporain en textes*, for additional literary readings.)

CHAPTER ORGANIZATION Each chapter of *Voix francophones* is divided into three parts. Each part opens with an authentic reading (***Texte***) followed by a quick comprehension check (***Vérification***) and an activity designed to elicit student opinion on the unit theme (***A votre avis***). Next, one discourse or writing hint is presented: ***Stratégies pour écrire*** (Part I), ***Regarder de près*** (Part II), ***Stratégies pour s'exprimer*** (Part III). This is reinforced immediately by a practical application of the strategy or hint using the earlier authentic text. The following ***Discussion*** section presents activities that delve more deeply into the issues and require students to demonstrate critical thinking skills. In the final stage, students are encouraged to go beyond the specifics presented in the articles and examine these issues as they relate to their own life experiences and their own culture (***Expansion***). Each unit concludes with an oral activity (debate, panel discussion, or role play) and a suggested written activity. These final activities serve as a synthesis for the two chapters of the unit (***Synthèse***).

WAYS TO USE *VOIX FRANCOPHONES*

FOR A CONVERSATION COURSE In a conversation course, the teacher may elect to omit the written assignments, use them to support the speaking skills, or have the students prepare the activities not in writing, but for oral presentation in class. The linguistic focus will be on the section entitled ***Stratégies pour s'exprimer***. The pace of the class (one unit every two or three weeks) allows time for students to give oral presentations, perform role plays, or hold debates. In addition, video news broadcasts may be easily incorporated into the course to reinforce listening skills and provide additional viewpoints and updates.

FOR A COMPOSITION COURSE In a composition course, the teacher may elect to omit some of the longer oral activities, use them as preparatory activities for writing assignments, or have students prepare written position papers offering their viewpoints. The linguistic focus will be on the two sections entitled ***Stratégies pour écrire*** and ***Regarder de près***. The first section is an organizational strategy usually at the discourse level, while the second is a brief reminder of a more technical aspect of writing. The pace of the class allows for some in-class writing, peer-editing, or computer-assisted writing options.

FOR A COMBINED COMPOSITION AND CONVERSATION COURSE In a combined composition and conversation course, *Voix francophones* gives teachers the opportunity to coordinate instructional efforts in both areas while providing a natural link through the unit themes. The composition and conversation skills are truly integrated and reinforce one another while maintaining the content focus of the course. Instruction in both skills can be contextualized and balanced, leaving time for the instructor to combine this text with a grammar reference or the corresponding reader.

FOR A FRANCOPHONE LITERATURE OR CULTURE COURSE *Voix francophones* may be used as a supplemental textbook in a course devoted to Francophone literature or culture. The themes and issues provide important background knowledge and offer insight into differing points of view in the contemporary Francophone world. The authentic texts provide an opportunity to introduce critical concepts to students and encourage discussion and an understanding before exploring these same issues through a literary text. For example, the unit on immigration raises important issues and concerns, while introducing the point of view of differing groups of immigrants (women) and second-generation immigrants (*les Beurs*). Upon completion of this unit, students are in a better position to read and more fully understand integral literary texts with immigration themes.

UNITE 1. LES ENJEUX DE LA FRANCOPHONIE

CHAPITRE 1. LE RAYONNEMENT CULTUREL DE LA FRANCE

This first chapter provides students with an introduction to the Francophone world and raises the important question of how a country the size of France has come to influence so many countries around the world.

A VOTRE AVIS (P. 9) Follow-up: Replace *La France* with *les Etats-Unis* and re-do the activity. Interesting discussions ensue, particularly for statement #4 (substituting *différents états* for *certains Etats africains*) and statements #5 and #6.

DISCUSSION (P. 11) Variation: This topic may be set up as a debate with groups of students explaining the cultural influence of these countries and predicting which country (countries) will carry a dominating influence into the twenty-first century.

DISCUSSION (P. 16) Variation: This topic may be explored as part of a student-designed opinion poll. Have students interview other students of French (from other courses) as homework and tabulate the results. What are the most commonly cited reasons why students of French at your institution have chosen to study French?

A VOTRE AVIS (P. 19) Follow-up: In light of the advantages and disadvantages of status as a *DOM ou TOM* of France, ask students to comment on their understanding of the advantages and disadvantages facing Puerto Rico in its relationship with the United States. Do students believe that Puerto Rico will one day become the fifty-first state? Are there any other regions that might someday be considered for statehood?

EXPANSION (P. 24) Follow-up: Ask students which country currently has the most influence on the United States (from a cultural point of view). This may be the focus of a discussion or debate between opposing views.

CHAPITRE 2. L'IDENTITE FRANCOPHONE ET L'IDENTITE NATIONALE: LES PROFILS MULTIPLES

This chapter reviews the origins of the term *la francophonie* and explores identity in Guadeloupe as expressed in poetry and identity in Quebec as revealed in an important opinion poll.

A VOTRE AVIS (P. 29) Follow-up: Ask students to what extent their native language is a critical part of their identity. Follow this with a discussion about the English-only movement in some parts of the United States. This may also be set up as a debate. Should the government require that all business be conducted in English, as the official language of the U.S., or should we recognize and support the use of other languages as individual expressions of cultural identity?

EXPANSION (PP. 35–36) Follow-up: Bring in (or have students bring in) to class other poems with themes of identity and feelings for one's homeland. Alternatively, ask students to write a poem expressing their own sense of identity or relationship to a particular place.

EXPANSION (P. 43) Follow-up: Have students assume the role of one of the five "portrait types" of *Québécois* described in the reading. Organize a debate focusing on the question of independence for the province of Quebec.

UNITE 2. L'ENVIRONNEMENT ET LA GESTION DE LA PLANETE

CHAPITRE 3. L'ENVIRONNEMENT: C'EST L'AFFAIRE DE TOUS!

This chapter identifies specific environmental concerns in France today, and concrete steps that have been taken in one major French city to combat these problems. In whom do the French place their confidence that these concerns will be addressed and solutions found?

A VOTRE AVIS (P. 54) Follow-up: To underscore the important link between physical geography and environmental concerns, ask students to select different regions of the U.S. and to identify specific environmental problems related to geography or industry in these regions.

DISCUSSION (P. 61) Follow-up: Have students compare their lists of priorities with others in the class. Is it difficult for everyone to agree on a set of priorities? Why or why not?

APPLICATION (P. 66) Follow-up: Which U.S. states have the most rigorous recycling programs or environmental policies? Why these states? Which states have no laws or mandatory recycling programs? Why these states?

CHAPITRE 4. FAIRE AVANCER LE MONDE, SANS FAIRE RECULER LA TERRE

This chapter raises the issue of environmental policies that may conflict with cultural values and traditions and explores two Francophone countries similar in size but facing entirely different environmental problems.

A VOTRE AVIS (P. 73) Variation: Each of these statements may be used as the basis of a debate. Divide the class into five groups and have each group select one statement. Have each group prepare to present both sides of each statement (agreeing with the statement or opposing it). Set a time limit for the debate of five minutes.

A VOTRE AVIS (P. 78) Follow-up: Question #4 raises a very controversial issue about the role of government in family planning. Have students compare policies in different countries (from the reading, and beyond; China, for example). This question might also be organized as a debate.

DISCUSSION (P. 79) Suggestion: May be organized as a debate. Individuals or teams of students lobby for more governmental support for particular medical needs.

Alternative: Focus on the issue of AIDS and the rapid spread of this deadly disease. What can be done to stop the spread of AIDS (see also ***Expansion***) and why, despite enormous educational efforts in the U.S., do some people continue to engage in unprotected sex?

EXPANSION (P. 87) Follow-up discussion: Recognizing the value of the slogan "Think globally, act locally," how will we ever solve truly global environmental problems without world-wide policies and laws? Who should/would establish and enforce such policies?

UNITE 3. IMMIGRATION: PERSPECTIVES MULTIPLES

CHAPITRE 5. EMIGRATION ET IMMIGRATION

This chapter explores the historical evolution and population patterns of immigrants to France and examines some of the reasons for current tensions between the French and recent immigrant groups to France. From yet another perspective, the first article offers a portrait of the French as immigrants to other countries. Where do they go? What do they do?

DISCUSSION (P. 96) Follow-up: Have students trace the historical patterns of different groups of immigrants to the United States. Why did these groups come at these specific points in history? Were the grandparents or great-grandparents of any students immigrants to this country? For what reasons did they choose the U.S.?

A VOTRE AVIS (P. 102) Suggestion: Question #3 focusing on different criteria for selected groups of immigrants would be the basis of an interesting debate.

DISCUSSION (P. 103) Follow-up: Raise the issue of immigration to the U.S. from Mexico. Increasingly in the news are the efforts of the U.S. government to maintain tighter control over the flow of immigrants into the southwest United States. Why is there so much recent attention focused on this issue? What policies should the U.S. follow in this situation? Why?

APPLICATION (P. 108) Suggestion: These topics may be presented as debates.

CHAPITRE 6. LA VOIX DES IMMIGRE(E)S

This chapter focuses on immigration from the point of view of the immigrant. What challenges or prejudices do immigrants face?

A VOTRE AVIS (P. 115) Follow-up: Ask students if they know any recent immigrants or any first-generation offspring of immigrants to the U.S. What has been their experience integrating into American society?

Alternative follow-up: Ask any foreign students in class (whether or not they intend to permanently stay in the U.S.) to describe their experiences and perceptions of how Americans have interacted with them since their arrival. Or invite an immigrant from the community to visit class and offer his/her perspective.

DISCUSSION (P. 116) Follow-up: The separation of church and state has been a recent issue in the U.S. in light of the question, "should prayer be permitted in public schools?" Set up a debate or discussion of this topic with students offering different opinions. Why does this subject raise such emotion in the U.S.? (Consider the issues of freedom of speech and freedom of religion).

EXPANSION (P. 131) Follow-up discussion question: Are interracial couples accepted in your community? What about the children resulting from such a union?

Additional follow-up discussion question: Should parents of one culture heritage be permitted to adopt and raise a child from a distinctly different cultural heritage? Why or why not?

UNITE 4. RELIGION: TRADITIONS, EVOLUTION, QUESTIONS

CHAPITRE 7. CE QUE CROIENT LES FRANÇAIS

This chapter examines religious affiliation and participation in religious ceremonies and observances of the French in contemporary France. The four largest religions in France are examined as well as the new age beliefs that go beyond traditional concepts of religion.

A VOTRE AVIS (P. 139) Follow-up: Are there similar patterns between age and religious practice that can be identified in the U.S. (or Canada)? What are possible explanations of these and other identifiable trends?

EXPANSION (P. 141) Follow-up: Subject for discussion or debate: television religious leaders (James Bakker, Pat Robertson, etc.), their scandals, and their political influence.

EXPANSION (P. 147) Follow-up discussion question: Are there any religions incompatible with a democratic society? How can widely varying religious practices and religious freedoms be preserved within a larger society?

A VOTRE AVIS (P. 151) Follow-up: With which of the new age practices mentioned in the article are you familiar? What do you believe will be the dominant religion or belief system in the year 2025? Why?

CHAPITRE 8. LA CONDITION FEMININE DANS UN MONDE ISLAMIQUE

This chapter offers a variety of perspectives on the role of women within an Islamic society.

A VOTRE AVIS (P. 167) Follow-up: Students may be surprised to learn that more and more young women are adopting the custom of wearing a veil. Ask them to identify behaviors in young people in this country that represent a return to an earlier practice (i.e., increase in church attendance by young people, growth of conservative political movements, etc.)

DISCUSSION (P. 174) Follow-up: Ask students for examples in American (and Canadian) society where there has been a reversal in perspective when women began to adopt certain roles (in the workplace, in advertising, etc.)

UNITE 5. VALEURS D'HIER, D'AUJOURD'HUI ET DE DEMAIN

CHAPITRE 9. AU SEUIL DE L'AN 2000: TENDANCES DES FRANÇAIS

This chapter offers a detailed look at societal values in France today and how they are perceived to have changed over time.

A VOTRE AVIS (P. 181) Follow-up: Have students conduct a poll (in class or as an outside assignment) based on the one presented on p. 179. Which values have lost importance in recent years and which ones have gained?

DISCUSSION (P. 183) Alternative: The list of important words would also make an interesting basis for a student opinion poll.

EXPANSION (P. 196) Follow-up discussion question: What role does the media play in the perception of happiness? How does television contribute to the desire for more material possessions? How does television alter our perceptions of self and others?

A VOTRE AVIS (P. 199) Follow-up debate question: Can the modern convenience of television "zapping" or "channel surfing" really influence our perception of reality and how we interact with one another?

CHAPITRE 10. REGARD SUR L'ACTUALITE AFRICAINE

This chapter offers a multitude of perspectives on what it means to be an African today and which values might be identified as characteristic of African society.

A VOTRE AVIS (P. 213) Follow-up: In what ways does the issue of respect for *pluralité des voies et des formes* also represent a concern for the U.S.?

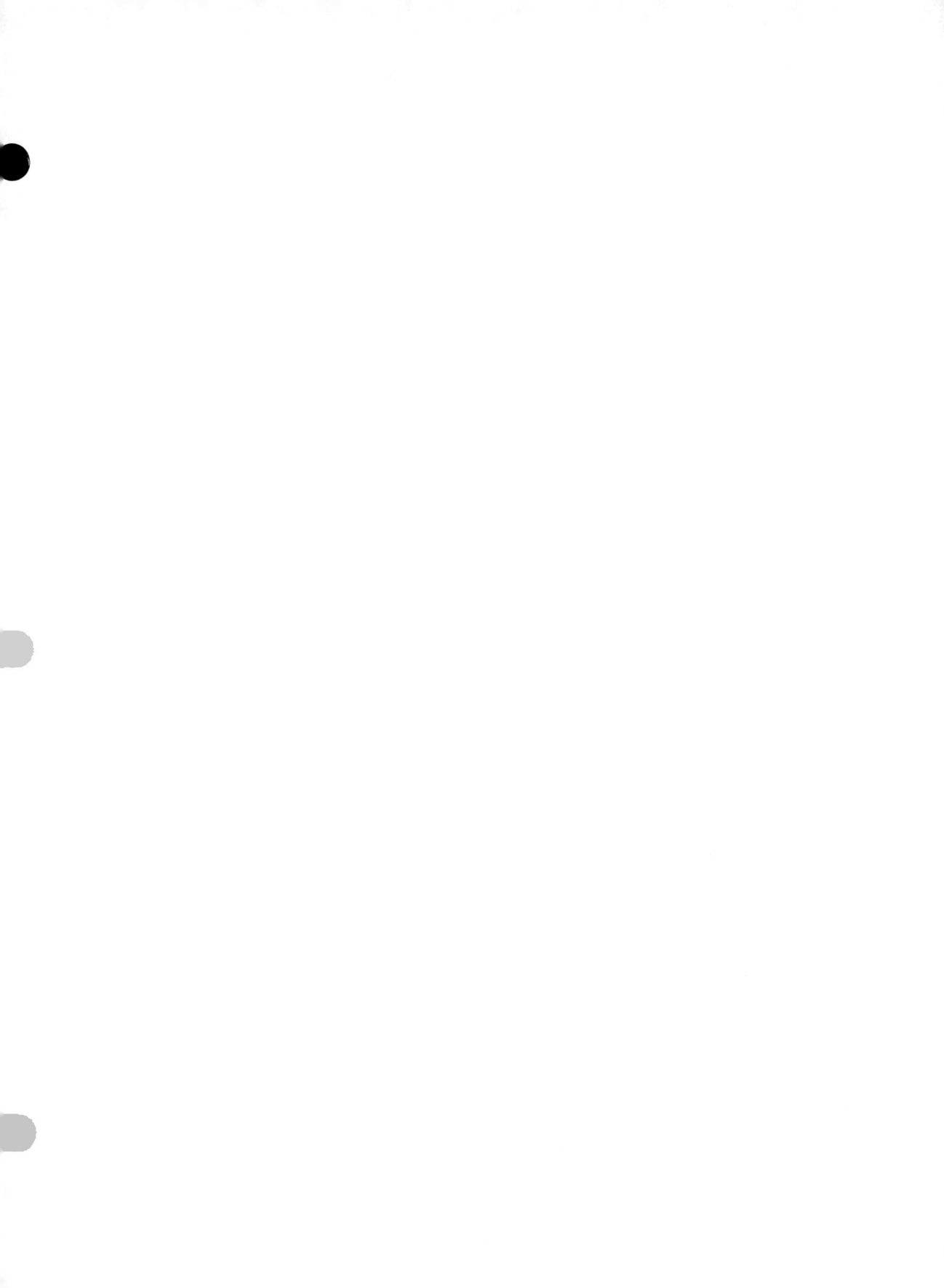